THE WORLD OF MUSIC

EDITED BY SIR GEORGE FRANCKENSTEIN, G.C.V.O., AND OTTO ERICH DEUTSCH

GERMAN SONG

MAYTIME
Song by Christoph Willibald Gluck
Page in colour lithography from a German song book, 1866

ELISABETH SCHUMANN

GERMAN SONG

*WITH 4 PLATES IN COLOUR
& 41 BLACK-AND-WHITE
ILLUSTRATIONS*

NEW YORK

CHANTICLEER PRESS

FIRST PUBLISHED 1948 BY

CHANTICLEER PRESS INC 41 EAST 50TH STREET NEW YORK

IN ASSOCIATION WITH

ADPRINT LTD LONDON

PRINTED IN HOLLAND
BY NEDERLANDSCHE ROTOGRAVURE LEIDEN

CONTENTS

PLATES IN COLOUR

MAYTIME
Song by Christoph Willibald Gluck
Page in colour lithography from a German song book, 1866
FRONTISPIECE

THE LORELEI ROCKS ON THE RHINE
Water-colour by Myles Birket Foster
Art Gallery, Glasgow
PAGE 19

FRANZ SCHUBERT
A posthumous portrait by an artist who was a close friend of Schubert
Oil painting by Wilhelm August Rieder, 1875. Schubert Museum, Vienna
PAGE 38

SCHUBERT AND HIS FRIENDS ON AN EXCURSION NEAR VIENNA
Water-colour by Leopold Kupelwieser, 1820
Schubert Museum, Vienna
PAGE 55

Acknowledgments are due to the following for the pictures reproduced on the pages mentioned:
COLOUR: 19 and 55, Glasgow Museum and Art Gallery; 38, Schubert Museum, Vienna
BLACK-AND-WHITE: 9, Bayerische Staatsbibliothek, Munich; 13, Universitätsbibliothek, Heidelberg; 25, Galerie des 19. Jahrhunderts, Belvedere, Vienna, and Messrs. Anton Schroll & Co., Vienna; 29, Photographische Gesellschaft, Berlin; 43, Städtische Sammlungen, Vienna

ILLUSTRATIONS IN BLACK & WHITE

The translation from Madame Schumann's manuscript in German is by D. Millar Craig

AUTHOR'S NOTE

This book makes no claim to be a comprehensive survey of the origin and development of German Song (which, for brevity's sake, I shall refer to simply as "Song" in the following pages), nor does it aim at tracing the course it has taken through the centuries, influenced as that has been by the spirit of the times and the advance of music as a whole. That voluminous chapter of the history of music has already been fully dealt with in more books than it would be easy to count. But, though I have not lost sight of the way in which my subject is bound up with the history of music itself, I have confined myself mainly to an analysis, as adequate as possible, of the poetry and music of a considerable number of the masterpieces of German song literature and the characteristics of their creators.

I

ALL THAT HAS LIFE AND BREATH

I F we are to penetrate at all deeply into the nature of song and the important place in the literature of music which rightly belongs to it, we must bring some scrutiny to bear on the perfected alliance of poetry and music which is song, and particularly on the nature of German lyric poetry, the foundation on which German song is built.

A conception of the union between the worlds of reality and of ideals through the medium of art has ruled German poetry from the earliest ages. German lyricism takes real life as its theme, and idealises it in poetic form. In it are manifest all worldly and religious experience, all the joys and griefs known to mankind, the love of Nature and of "all that has life and breath", of everything sublime and eternal, side by side with the simple emotions of hearth and home. As the poet Uhland has expressed it, "they sing of all things lovely that human hearts delight, they sing of all things lofty that human souls excite". Everything artificial, invented, affected, is banned from it, and truth is its first commandment. It is on that truth that the worth of song and poetry rests.

Goethe said of his own poems, "there is in them nothing which has not been lived, felt, enjoyed, suffered, as part of experience". That might be said as truly of almost all the German lyric poets: the poems of Rückert, Lenau, Uhland, Geibel, Chamisso, Heyse, Mörike, Eichendorff, Heine, and the rest, are poetic confessions of their writers' inmost beings. Their idiom, even in its moments of deepest emotion, is of the utmost simplicity and homeliness, never artificial or involved. The flow of their own intrinsic rhythm, besides, makes them ideally fitted for wedding to music. While reading them, and especially while reading them aloud, even the least musical must feel that the words were conceived as though already linked with music. A sympathy with music is almost always manifest; that is the secret of the fascination they have exercised on composers.

There is one exception, however, in the indifference to music of Goethe himself. As the greatest of German poets, whose words have a music all their own, he has always exercised a magnetic influence on song composers of his own and later ages. Schubert composed nearly a hundred of his poems, and Hugo Wolf some fifty. Yet Goethe had himself no critical judgment of music. Schubert's setting of his 'Erl King', for instance, made no impression on him; only in his old age did he revise his opinion of it when it was sung to him with irresistible artistry by Schröder-Devrient.

Even then, however, he betrayed no great understanding of what music can mean; he said, "I once heard that composition long ago, and it made no impression on me, but when presented like that it becomes a veritable picture". So slight an appreciation had one whose own poems are like streams of music, and on whom one would expect music to have had so strong an influence.

He makes his Wilhelm Meister say, for instance, "To me it is as though a hidden spirit whispered rhythmically, so that as I go afoot I walk in measures and hear in them soft tones which accompany my steps, like a melody once heard with pleasure in other days and scenes". His Werther tells us, too, "Not a word of the olden powers of music's magic seems to me improbable". Mendelssohn's music, tender and insinuating, appealed to Goethe far more than did bold conceptions like Schubert's 'Erl King' or the revolutionary grandeur of Beethoven.

The great composers, on the other hand, were all along quick to recognise the power of Goethe, looking up to his genius, as they did, with sincere reverence. Schubert was only a lad of seventeen when he embarked on his inspired settings of Goethe's poetry, with 'Gretchen am Spinnrade' as the first. In the course of his eighteenth year he composed a round dozen of Goethe's texts, five of them actually in one day, the enchanting 'Heidenrös-lein' among them. That Goethe failed so completely to recognise Schubert's significance and to appreciate at its true worth the enthusiasm with which the younger man surrendered himself to the spell of Goethe's poetry, is the more to be deplored as it kept him from realising how great was his own influence on Schubert's creative powers and thus on the whole course of the development of modern art song. To trace that development, however, we must turn back to a much earlier day.

From the pages of history we can learn how song has always been treasured in Germany as part of her people's heritage. In the earlier centuries of the Christian era, we find the Church borrowing the people's songs and adapting them to its services; the development of harmonised song is largely due to Church influence.

Secular song, however, could look for no other encouragement from the Church, and in the feudal ages it was the minstrels, in court or hall, or at gatherings of humbler folk, who kept the art alive. In most cases a poet as well as a musician, the minstrel made his own verses and set them to music of his own devising, borrowing only occasionally from older sources. His is an art which has even now not wholly disappeared. Until quite recent times, villagers gathered of an evening in the inn might hear the songs of old heroic deeds, of "battles long ago" chanted by a grey-haired singer of the roads, to his own guitar accompaniment. Records of such minstrelsy, moreover, one as old as the eighth century, are still preserved in German libraries. These are ballads, however, rather than songs in lyric form; in Germany the first foundations of art song as we know it now were laid in the age of Chivalry, of jousts and tournaments, by the minstrel knights who took the name of Minnesingers.

Wagner, with his lofty indifference to the anachronisms in which it might involve him, brought a representative gathering of them together for the song contest which is the second act of his *Tannhäuser*. His personages there are real figures of history, and Wolfram von Eschenbach was one of the most illustrious. It was on his version of the Grail legend that Wagner founded the text of his *Parsifal*. Walther von der Vogelweide was another; it was he whom the Walther of the *Meistersinger* claimed as his teacher when facing his trial for admission to the Guild. Tannhäuser, too, was a real personage, like others of the minstrel knights a valiant Crusader, and in no way akin to his purely legendary namesake of the Venusberg with whom Wagner was rash enough to identify him.

The song with which Wolfram, in the opera, opens the contest is no unfair parody of the Minnesingers' art. "Minne" means "love", but "worship" is a fitter term for the theme which the knights extolled—a fantastic homage to their ladies, set forth in florid mixed metaphor. Some of the melodies are still extant; like the shaping of the verses, they betray the influence of the Troubadours on the other side of the Rhine. Formal, even stilted, as they must seem to modern ears, they show, none the less, how far the twelfth and thirteenth centuries had carried the art of song from its primitive beginnings. More than one collection of Minnesinger songs may still be studied; one, at Jena, includes a song, with its melody, by Walther von der Vogelweide.

As feudal power declined, and wealth and influence came into the hands of burghers, merchants and craftsmen, the Minnesingers made way in the next centuries for the Mastersingers. How they acquired or adopted that

MASTER HEINRICH FRAUENLOB
Illumination from the Manesse Codex of Minnesingers, c. 1340

HANS SACHS
From a Nuremberg handbill of the late sixteenth century

name is no longer known; "master" denoted a definite grade to which a craftsman rose from his beginnings as apprentice, a Mastersinger being normally one who had reached that summit in his trade. But the name implied, too, a mastery not merely of singing but of composing songs, words and music, a mastery awarded, as a degree is granted, only on the passing of a test. Again it is to Wagner that we owe a lifelike picture of the period; his one comic opera gives a faithful view of the Mastersingers and their art.

The first of them, or, as some would have it, the last of the Minnesingers, has always been known in Germany as "Frauenlob" though his name was Heinrich von Meissen. Early in the fourteenth century he founded a guild of singers at Mainz, and before long the example was enthusiastically followed in other cities. That Nuremberg holds pride of place among them is due not only to Wagner, but to Hans Sachs himself, the outstanding poet of his age. So prolific was he that thirty-four bulky volumes are needed to hold what remains of his poems, more than six thousand of them. Mainly on scriptural subjects, and set to melodies often borrowed from the Minnesingers or from the Church, they include, too, songs on secular themes; in 1560, when he was sixty-five, his first wife, Kunigunde, died, and several of his poems of that year are mournings for his loss.

Der
Meisterliche Hort/
in vier gekrönten Thönen.
Das Erste Gesetz/
im langen Thon Heinrich Müglings.

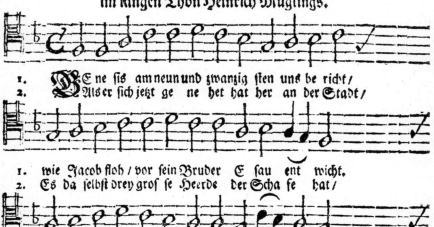

1. WEne sis am neun und zwanzig sten uns be richt/
2. Als er sich jetzt ge ne het hat her an der Stadt/

1. wie Jacob floh / vor sein Bruder E sau ent wicht.
2. Es da selbst drey grosse Heerde der Schafe hat/

1. Daß er in Me so po ta mi am kom men.
2. Jacob fragt um Bericht; als er ein ge nommen

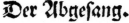

Der Abgesang.

die ses Or tes Ge le gen heit/
Sie sag ten ja mit gutem Bescheid/

A SONG OF THE MASTERSINGERS
From Joh. Chr. Wagenseil's 'Von der Meistersinger holdseligen Kunst', 1697

THE SINGERS
Woodcut by Jost Amman, 1568

None of his nor, indeed, any of the Mastersingers' songs was simple enough to take its place in the national body of folk-song; they were hedged about by just such a pedantic code of rules as David and Kothner expound to the bewildered Walther in the first act of Wagner's opera. So precise were the laws as to leave but little freedom to poet or singer, and with few exceptions the mastersongs are cast in a uniform mould. Carried to ridiculous lengths though it was, however, the jealous guardianship of the art gave the nation a renewed sense of the value of song as a possession to be treasured.

Side by side with these developments of formal song, and largely independent of them, folk-song went its own way, springing uncultivated from the soil in which it was rooted, the hearts of a simple music-loving folk.

PSALM-SINGING IN CHURCH
Sixteenth-century woodcut illustrating the words of St. Paul (Col. iii. 16)

Like the old minstrels' ballads, it was drawn at first from history or legend, glorifying great deeds of bygone days. But little by little simpler themes made their way into it, and many which have come down to us are love songs. Students, as early as the sixteenth century, had songs of their own, and several crafts and societies played their part in adding to the store. Many of the folk-songs even of that date, almost invariably strophic in form and rhymed, are obviously the models on which later art songs were composed.

Though frowned on for hundreds of years by the Church, these songs of the people had their revenge; many of the most impressive chorale and hymn tunes now in regular use in sacred music were adopted from folk-song. The chorale 'O Haupt voll Blut und Wunden' (O Sacred Head surrounded) in Bach's *St. Matthew Passion* was originally a secular love song, and the services of Roman Catholic and Protestant churches have many another instance of folk-song turned to the uses of worship. Even tunes which were originally dance measures have been adapted to sacred uses.

If that was the first stage in bridging the gap between folk-song and the art song as we know it to-day, it was carried farther by composers of the contrapuntal school in the sixteenth century, notably by the two Fincks, Heinrich and his great-nephew Hermann, professor and organist at Wittenberg University. Their treatment of folk-song, however, lent it a complexity wholly foreign to its own simple conciseness. Its rescue was due in large measure to Italian influence, and the credit should be given to the composer Hans Leo Hassler. Learning his art in Venice, he was for a time a protégé of the great mercantile house of Fugger in Augsburg, and afterwards organist of a Nuremberg church. His sacred and secular songs did much to import something of Italian grace and lightness to German melody, and to give back to folk-song some likeness to its national conciseness of form.

Not until the early years of the seventeenth century, however, did songs for a single voice begin to have a place of their own as creations of studied art, and at first they were all designed for sacred use. It was a sad period for German secular poetry; its old simplicity, alike of feeling and expression, had given way to a vapid sentimentality, set forth in florid, artificial verse. But sturdy German common sense could not long endure such travesties of the native genius, and before the middle of the century men like Heinrich Albert were composing songs which reflected the true taste of their country. A poet as well as a musician, Albert was a nephew of Heinrich Schütz, whose eminence would demand a place even in this brief summary, were it not that his work was mainly outside the realm of song. Oratorio and cantata were the forms he cultivated. These, along with opera, were the next form of competition encountered by song; they were winning so large a share of popular favour as to oust the simple song from the place which is its own by right. How wholly song, as such, had fallen into neglect is obvious when we recall that neither Bach nor Handel showed much interest in it. Bach, it is true, did leave us a number of songs, sacred and secular, for a single voice, but they are for the most part in the style of the Protestant chorale; as to Handel, he wrote only a few songs of no great significance.

Not till the second half of the eighteenth century did a new interest in song emerge, probably as a reaction from the popularity of the aria, particularly the Italian aria. Several composers turned with enthusiasm to

The Lorelei Rocks on the Rhine
Water-colour by Myles Birket Foster
Art Gallery, Glasgow

setting the newly awakened lyric poetry; among them Goethe's friends, Reichardt and Zelter, must be given honourable mention, as well as Zumsteeg, whose songs, as we know, appealed to Schubert in his boyhood's days. They were the first who strove to embody the symmetry and simplicity of verse structure in the music they composed for it, and, as far as lay within their power, to maintain a kinship between poetry and music. Lack of creative individuality, with a poverty of melodic and harmonic invention, kept them, certainly, from rising above a mere scholarly correctness, so that their songs have now little more than historical interest for us.

On a vastly higher plane are the songs of Haydn, Mozart, and Beethoven, belonging more or less to the same era. But, alas, how few they are! These songs do not reach that summit to which a few decades later those of Schubert mounted, but, though the element of folk-song, or what we ought more correctly to call the national idiom of song, is prominent in their conception, they did, none the less, serve, as only works of genius can, as the models for the song composition of the following century.

It was not so much the songs of these composers, however, as their opera and oratorio arias that gave a lead to succeeding generations. While Haydn in his songs, largely because of their mediocre texts, left us little of real worth (there are a very few exceptions like 'She never told her Love'), his arias in *The Creation* and *The Seasons* must have had some influence on Schubert's song-writing. The same is no doubt true of Mozart's arias in his operas, with their enchanting melody and deft characterisation. But his songs, too—'An Chloë', 'Abendempfindung', and best of all, the beloved 'Veilchen' (Violet)—have a classic beauty of their own. In that last, particularly, Mozart's sincerity and the finished beauty of Goethe's verse blend into a unity of compelling charm. That it is not set in strict form, but rather after the style of a ballad, and so is not on consistent lines throughout, actually adds to its charm. But for the development of song into any new form, Mozart can no more be given credit than Haydn.

Nor can Beethoven; the smaller forms of music are not well adapted to such titanic genius as his; he left only a few songs. He was the first, however, to extend the bounds of song; his *Sechs Geistliche Lieder* (Six Sacred Songs) form the earliest song-cycle we possess, with 'An die ferne Geliebte' taking a noble place beside it. But while these and the broadly conceived 'Adelaide' are rather in the style of arias, Beethoven did write a number of songs which have their place among the most beautiful in the whole literature. Among his greatest achievements are the settings of Goethe's poems. 'Wonne der Wehmut', 'Mit einem gemalten Band', 'Neue Liebe, neues Leben',

'Mailied' and the two songs for Clärchen in his *Egmont* music, though these last are, strictly speaking, arias.

If Beethoven, as song composer, did not rise to such heights as in his large-scale music, he was, no less than Haydn and Mozart, a guiding light and a pathfinder for Schubert. The fervour of his religious faith, the irresistible surge of his love songs ('Freudvoll und leidvoll', 'Adelaide'), as well as his daring innovations in form and the virtuosic shaping of the pianoforte accompaniment as an integral part of the song, all contribute to the outstanding importance of his work. Beethoven's influence can be clearly traced in the very earliest of Schubert's songs, notably in the technically difficult accompaniments of 'Gretchen am Spinnrade', 'Rastlose Liebe' and 'Erlkönig'.

While he adopted as his models the three great masters, Haydn, Mozart and Beethoven, for all of whom he cherished a sincere veneration, Schubert was no less truly at one with the poetry of Goethe. Half by instinct, half by conscious application, he grasped the essence of the melodious words and their musical rhythm, achieving that ideal union of word and tone which imparts the deeper meaning of music to poetry. That, as all the world knows, Schubert attained even in his earliest essays in a way which has never been surpassed; it is with every right that he is held in honour as the creator of the modern German art song.

VIGNETTE FROM THE TITLE-PAGE
OF LUDWIG TIECK'S 'MINNELIEDER'
Etching by Philipp Otto Runge, 1803

II

MELODY, GAIETY, PASSION AND TEARS

NOT only as one of the greatest classical masters of all-round musical achievement, but also and above all as the most fertile, many-sided, and imaginatively gifted composer of German song of all time—so do we acclaim Franz Schubert. His spirit and his work could not be more fittingly crystallised in words than in Liszt's homage:

"Melody, gaiety, grace, reveries, passion, solace, tears, and flames streamed from the depths and heights of your heart; you make us well-nigh forget the greatness of your mastery in the enchantment of your spirit."

Schubert is for us the very embodiment of the spirit of music. Whatever he saw, whatever touched him, was transmuted to music. It must have been so. How else could we believe that within the span of only fourteen years, from his seventeenth year to his thirty-first, in which he died, he composed more than six hundred songs as well as countless masterworks of every order in forms both great and small! Even that achievement, incredible as it may well seem, is surpassed by his complete grasp, musical and spiritual, of the poems of Goethe's maturity, and by his success in setting them to music in a perfection of form which has never been bettered And that in his seventeenth year.

MARGARET AT THE SPINNING-WHEEL
Lithograph by Eugène Delacroix from a French edition of Goethe's 'Faust', 1828

Consider the very first of the Goethe songs he composed, 'Gretchen
am Spinnrade' (Margaret at the Spinning-Wheel). Schubert employed a
rondo-like form for it, a consistent setting of its ten four-line verses. While
the voice part, with its emotion and deft characterisation, changes the melody
almost imperceptibly in each section, it maintains its rhythm from the first
to the last bar. The steady sextuplet motion of the accompaniment presents
the hum of the turning wheel in a way that could not well be clearer; so
has Schubert depicted every stage in Gretchen's emotion, rising to the verge
of crazed intensity and then sinking almost to numbness. The mental picture
is vividly true to life. How magical is the transition to a parallel key at the
words "His lofty mien, his noble form", and what a touch of genius at the

moment of tensest feeling with the words "And oh, his kiss", to interrupt the sextuplets in the accompaniment, to show that the wheel has stopped, and then to let it begin again haltingly and unevenly! And what a depth of feeling is revealed by the repetition at the very end of the song, of the words "My peace is gone, my heart is sad", though the original poem ends with the words "To be lost in his arms".

In the song 'Rastlose Liebe' (Restless Love), Schubert employed a like technique, keeping the rhythm steady to the end, and illustrating the song's emotion by the unvarying semiquaver movement in the accompaniment. It is a device which he turned to good account in almost all his songs of which movement is a feature—'Erlkönig', for instance, with its hoof beats in the triplets of the pianoforte part, or the two songs 'Wohin?' and 'Liebes-botschaft' with their accompaniments illustrating the flowing brook. In 'Die Forelle' (The Trout), too, the dashing to and fro of the little fish in the water is presented with unerring sureness of effect.

In these and many other songs Schubert, following Beethoven's example, gives us accompaniments which are no mere backgrounds for the voice, but integral parts of the songs, with preludes and codas making their independent effect. That did not deter him from demanding virtuosic attainments from the pianist, and 'Erlkönig' has forced many a one to devise some simplification. Schubert, so we are told, did so once himself, answering the singer's raillery with the remark, "Let others tackle the triplets, they are too hard for me". But his gift for depicting movement in his music is nowhere more obvious than in 'Die Forelle' where we cannot fail to visualise the swimming of the fish from the surface to the depths of the stream.

In his songs that go briskly forward he has almost always indicated a tempo for the opening, leaving it to the singer's artistic sense to introduce slightly slower moments where the words demand it. Likewise in the broadly conceived songs, like 'Du bist die Ruh', 'Im Abendrot', 'An die Musik', 'Ave Maria' and others, only the opening tempo is indicated; he no doubt took it for granted that the monumental calm of such songs would not be disturbed by wayward changes. One of the most magical of these songs is 'Im Abendrot' (At Sunset), with its words proclaiming a devout love of God and of His world, and its music obviously wrung from the depths of Schubert's spirit. The voice floats above arpeggios, tender as the tones of chorale or harp: as though lit by the rays of sunset at the words 'Irre sein an dir und mir' they seem to bear us up to celestial heights. In 'Du bist die Ruh' (Thou art Repose), a reserve which shuns any erotic thought calls up an image of the purest love.

'ERL KING'
Oil painting by Moritz von Schwind, c. 1840

While these, and the songs whose charm is in their gaiety of spirit, reflect Schubert's own sunny temperament, we have to admit that they are surpassed by the dramatic songs in the gifts of genius that they reveal. These in their overwhelming power can not only stand beside Hugo Wolf's songs of a like order, but even take rank above them in their lofty simplicity. 'Erlkönig', 'Prometheus', 'Grenzen der Menschheit', 'Die Stadt', 'Aufenthalt', 'Atlas', 'Gruppe aus dem Tartarus', 'Die Allmacht', are indeed songs of such power.

Schubert's astonishing versatility enabled him, too, to find profoundly affecting music for the gentler aspects of death. 'Der Tod und das Mädchen' (Death and the Maiden) is his best-known song of that order, but 'Der Jüngling und der Tod', 'Nachtstück' and 'Schwanengesang', though not so often heard, are treasures of no less worth. In the first two of these the words of Death are accompanied by chords like organ tones, while in 'Nachtstück' the old man dies amid the sound of harps, and in 'Schwanengesang' Death is transfigured in ethereal-sounding chords like those of muted strings.

THE YOUNG NOBLEMAN AND THE MILLER'S DAUGHTER
Woodcut by Ludwig Richter from 'Deutsches Balladenbuch', 1852

Serious texts attracted him most strongly; even his merry songs have often a veil of wistfulness. Humour and comedy are almost never found in his songs, and we know from sayings of his own that he thought them no fit subjects for music. It is the tragic songs which have the strongest hold on our affections, and which came from the heart of the composer. An entry in his diary says: "What I produce is due to my understanding of music and to my sorrows."

His widest success was won with the *Die schöne Müllerin* cycle, in which a tragic love story is set to music, and the heavy-hearted songs of *Winterreise* (Winter Journey) and *Schwanengesang* (The Swan Song). That name, by the way, was given to his last fourteen songs not by Schubert himself, but by his publisher.

Winterreise is no more than a series of mood pictures of an unhappy lover; *Die schöne Müllerin* (The Fair Maid of the Mill), on the other hand, presents a story in serial order. Here, in outline, is the tale. A miller's apprentice goes out into the world, and a brooklet leads him to a mill. He takes service with the miller there, and loses his heart to the miller's daughter.

The first four songs tell us of his wanderings, of the brook, and life in the mill. In the fifth to the ninth songs the bliss of young love is set forth; its unclouded happiness in the tenth to the twelfth. But then a dashing huntsman comes on the scene and wins the maiden's heart, supplanting the young miller; overcome by grief and jealousy, the unhappy lad throws himself into the stream, to find in it eternal peace. Schubert presents the stages of the tragedy in strophic songs of simply varied shape, and, in some, by straightforward settings. An apt folk-song atmosphere prevails throughout, and there could be no more abiding memorial to the poet Wilhelm Müller than Schubert has raised to him.

But besides those cycles in sombre mood, we have many other songs in which Schubert sings to us of joyous, lovely, cherished, and abiding things. His name can conjure up thoughts of blue skies, of sunshine, moon and stars; all these he enshrined in his music. The poet Mayrhofer has expressed this truth for us in words which his friend Schubert set to music in the enchanting song 'Geheimnis' (Secret):

"Say who made thee a singer so tender and so sweet,
    To draw down heaven's blessings the earth's dull cares to meet?
    In mist and vapour shrouded but erst the country lay;
    Yet spring's delight and sunshine thy songs to us convey."

(*Trans. by Eric Blom.*)

THE MILLER'S DAUGHTER REPENTS
Woodcut by Ludwig Richter, 1853

III

THE TENDER HEART

ORN thirteen years after Schubert, Schumann survived him by twenty-eight years, and we are inclined to think of them as contemporaries, though in fact Schumann did not seriously turn to composition till after Schubert had died.

Their names are often quoted together like those of Bach and Handel or of Haydn, Mozart and Beethoven, as representing one era of art, and as though their music revealed some kinship, mental and spiritual. Their works are actually as unlike as their temperaments were at opposite extremes. How many passages there are in Haydn's music which might be taken for Mozart's, and how many in Beethoven's early work which only an expert can distinguish from Mozart's, even as Schubert often reminds us of Mozart! In Schumann's, on the other hand, there is nowhere a single bar which anyone would ascribe to Schubert. It says much for Schumann's strong individuality that he went his own way uninfluenced by his enthusiasm for Schubert. That he did so was due, naturally, to the wide divergence between his outlook on the world, with his enlightened culture, and Schubert's.

The differences come to light most clearly in their songs; it is in them that objective experience and subjective feeling find their truest expression. Schubert was endowed with a naturally lighthearted temperament of no great complexity, accepting all that came his way, even material troubles, in a carefree spirit. Schumann was all his life a thinker, probing to the heart of life's problems; mental trouble did not overtake him, as is often assumed, only in his latter years and as the result of overburdening cares, but was present even in his early youth. He was only in his eighteenth year when he wrote to a friend, "This world and its people, what are they! A monstrous graveyard of strangled dreams, a garden of cypress and weeping willows, a silent peepshow with mournful figures".

Such was the young Schumann's view of life almost before he had passed its threshold, and before he knew anything of its material cares. Schubert, though he found himself in needy straits throughout his life, and with many a bitter disappointment to bear, never let his own bright spirits be clouded for long; he had Viennese blood in his veins, loved the Viennese dance music, all that he knew of the wide world's endless interest, and above all, his "holde Kunst", his noble art. So wide a divergence of character reveals itself, inevitably, in their music, and most of all in their songs.

ROBERT AND CLARA SCHUMANN
Lithograph by Eduard Kaiser, 1847

FRIEDRICH RÜCKERT
Crayon drawing by Karl Barth, c. 1833

Their choice of texts alone is a clear index of their differing thought and feeling. Schubert, in his amazing versatility, seized on poetry of almost every order—merry, grave, lyrical, dramatic, elegiac, and mystical. The great majority of the poems which Schumann set are lyrically romantic. Characteristic is his leaning towards the tender and gentle, even tragic, moods, towards spiritual grief turning to introspection or resignation.

A typical instance is the Heine song 'Schöne Wiege meiner Leiden'. Its theme has some kinship with the same poet's 'Der Doppelgänger' (The Double), which Schubert set to music. But what a world of difference there is between the two songs! With the simplest of means and in the strictest song form, Schubert has created a breath-taking mood-picture, in which the pianissimo chords of the opening mount in stride after stride to a three-fold fortissimo, to fall back at last to the sinister quiet of the beginning. In the Schumann song passion is held strongly in check; the tender close in a mood of resignation and the long, dreamy epilogue for the pianoforte lend it an almost lyrical character.

HEINRICH HEINE
Etching by Ludwig Emil Grimm, 1827

It would lead too far to quote all the Schumann songs in which tragic texts are set in tender strains of submission. It must suffice to recall such passages as "Nur Eine kennt meinen Schmerz" in the song 'Und wüssten's die Blumen' from the *Dichterliebe* cycle, the setting of the last words in 'Dein Angesicht' and the song 'Tief im Herzen trag ich Pein'. In only a few songs like 'Ich grolle nicht', 'Melancholie', and in the ballads, has Schumann sounded tones of power, and even these fall short of the realism in the Schubert and Hugo Wolf songs of dramatic force.

If our view of Schumann as a truly lyrical composer needs confirmation, we find it in his choice of texts for the majority of his songs, and especially for the best of them; they are almost all taken from the out-and-out romantics. Most of them come from Rückert and Heine; then follow, in diminishing order, Goethe (but there, too, only his more romantic poems), Eichendorff, Burns, Kerner, Lenau, Chamisso, and one or two others represented by only one song each. It is such purely lyrical songs which reveal Schumann's gifts at their best, and win for him his place among the greatest composers of German song. The enchanting tenderness and delicacy of songs like 'Der Nussbaum', 'Mondnacht', 'Die Lotosblume', 'Du bist wie eine Blume', and a number of others which are more nearly in folk-song idiom, like 'Marien-würmchen', 'Volksliedchen' and 'An den Sonnenschein', earn for them a place all their own.

In some of his less well-known songs Schumann achieved impressive effects by their masterly declamation; it is these which make it easy to understand how Hugo Wolf, master as he was himself of musical declamation, regarded Schumann as his model. 'Der Page', 'Die Kartenlegerin' and 'Meine Rose' are examples of finished craftsmanship in that domain.

On another lofty summit among Schumann's songs stands the cycle *Frauen-Liebe und Leben* (Woman's Love and Life). For that poetic idealisation of woman as wife and mother Schumann found such simple and yet deeply emotional music that I shall quarrel with none who counts the series as the best of all song-cycles.

Dichterliebe (a title we owe to Schumann himself) consists in settings of poems from Heine's *Buch der Lieder*, and in my view is not on the same high level as *Frauen-Liebe und Leben*. Side by side with songs which win our affection there are weaker numbers in it where the lyric purity is tainted by the poet's irony. Schumann's heart and mind were too tender for the expression of moods of that order. And while he was incapable of giving such thoughts the musical expression they demand, he let himself be betrayed in some of the others into banalities which stand out glaringly beside the finely conceived romantic songs of the cycle. 'Ein Jüngling liebt ein Mädchen' and 'Aus alten Märchen' are instances of the student-song mediocrity which seems to me a lapse from his own standard.

It is truer of him than of any other of the great song composers that his works include some weaker efforts, songs which are never heard. In his first year of song-composing he wrote nearly a hundred and fifty; the two cycles discussed above were among them, comprising twenty-four songs, along with *Myrthen* and the cycle of Eichendorff's songs, and literally dozens of single songs. Such a hot-house forcing of his inspiration might well produce a proportion of weaklings. It is no really damning criticism of a great master that we point to occasional weakness in his work. It should, on the contrary, serve to counter the charge often levelled against Schumann, that he was no very prolific composer, which is far from just. If his music has never won quite the universal affection given to the music of some others, it is no doubt because some of it is not easy to understand without careful study.

The great merit of his achievement rests on his having been the first of the intellectuals among the great composers; by his own profound knowledge and wide culture, he was able to raise the standard of musical appreciation to a higher level than it had reached before. He prepared the way, moreover, by infusing something of spirituality into the music of song, for its further development at the hands of Schubert's followers, most notably of Brahms and Hugo Wolf. His stature is far greater than that of any of his contemporaries, Mendelssohn, Franz, Jensen, Cornelius, and the rest. Their work was for the most part based so firmly on the tradition of folk-song or the elementary Protestant chorale, that it might have brought the development of song to a halt, had not Schumann's commanding spirit pointed to new paths. He expressed something of his discernment in the prophetic words, "To me it often seems as though we were face to face with new beginnings, as though we could strike chords which none had heard before."

IV

A SPIRIT MERGED IN NATURE'S

EW beginnings of which Schumann cannot have dreamed have made their way into music since he made that prophecy—whole-tone, quarter-tone, twelve-tone scales, atonality, and "chords which none had heard before". What he foresaw must have been new possibilities of progress along the lines laid down by the great masters. He cannot have guessed that the first steps towards fulfilment of his dreams of the future would be taken in his own day; his amazement can well be imagined when, three years before his death, the twenty-year-old Johannes Brahms played to him his first essays in composition, with their stern regard for classical tradition infused by new deeps of emotional expression. Schumann was so carried away by the music and by the modest, though self-assured, personality of the young man, as to hail him in an article in his own musical journal as "the Messiah of Music".

It proved to be an ill-omened saying; its tone of over-enthusiasm did a great deal to inflame the animosity towards him which was already rising among those younger spirits in the world of music who were surrendering to the sway of Liszt and Wagner, looking on Schumann himself as outmoded. None the less there were coteries which gathered staunchly round Schumann and Brahms, and an open feud between two factions followed inevitably. It endured for a long time and gave way at last only as Brahms's music continued to win an ever wider success and to encounter less opposition than the innovations which others strove to propagate. Now, and indeed for many years past, Brahms has taken his assured place by the side of the greatest masters, and his music has won its way to the farthest parts of the world. His popularity rests in large measure on his songs, of which there are more than three hundred.

In the very first, written between his eighteenth and twentieth years, he made it clear, just as Schubert did, that he possessed ideal gifts of genius for that form of composition. Though these songs may not be measured by the standard of the ripe achievement of his later years, they do reveal the characteristic features of his art in a degree which might well lead us, did we not know the date of their birth, to ascribe them to a much older Brahms.

'Liebestreu' and 'Weit über das Feld' are instances of that early maturity. Both songs display alike his depth of feeling and his twofold leaning

JOHANNES BRAHMS
Crayon drawing by Olga von Miller

towards the lyrically romantic and the tragically dramatic. 'Liebestreu' (Love's Faith) bears witness, too, to the sedate restraint to which he adhered in all his songs. Without losing this restraint for a single bar, he does achieve a remarkable characterisation and a complete contrast between the words of mother and daughter. In 'Weit über das Feld' Brahms employed, as he so often did, the form of varied strophic song, and by the slightest of variations in the last verse conveyed a bewitching dramatic effect.

'Spanisches Lied' is another of his first songs which must be mentioned; it is on a poem afterwards set by Hugo Wolf—the well-known 'In dem Schatten meiner Locken'. No one can fail to be struck by the way in which Brahms's setting, though not on the same high plane as that of the mature Wolf, does capture the same sense of warm colouring and make use of the same rhythm.

ᴛʜᴇ Fᴜʟʟ Mᴏᴏɴ
Oil painting by Caspar David Friedrich, c. 1820

From other youthful songs I must quote the lively 'Nachtigallen schwin-
gen', 'Juchhe' (strongly influenced though it is by Mendelssohn) and the
Volkskinderlieder (Children's Folk-Songs) of a rather later date ('Sandmänn-
chen' and 'Wiegenlied' among them), as well as other folk-songs which
Brahms afterwards revised. Best-loved among the last are 'Mein Mädel hat
einen Rosenmund', 'Feinsliebchen, du sollst mir nicht barfuss gehn', 'Da
unten im Tale', though these are not by any means alone in their compelling
charm.

From his earliest youth Brahms was devoted to his country's folk-song,
and among his first songs are many folk-song arrangements; in his later
work, too, folk-song melodies are often turned to account, while others of
his songs are in what might be called folk-song idiom. Such, for instance, are 'Sonntag' ("So hab ich doch die ganze Woche"), 'Wiegenlied',

'Sommerabend', 'Vergebliches Ständchen', several maidens' songs, 'Der Jäger' and 'Der Schmied' (The Blacksmith), among others. In the accompaniment to the last song, the suggestion of hammer strokes and leaping sparks is particularly effective.

'An eine Äolsharfe' (To an Aeolian Harp), on a poem by Mörike, belongs almost to the same period and might well be described as the first song of Brahms's maturity. In contrast to Hugo Wolf's treatment of it, he has given the song a more compact shape and, by the recitatives at the beginning and in the middle section, lent it something of *arioso* character. It reveals, like many another song, Brahms's strong leaning towards the romantic. To this tendency, too, the next song series, op. 32, bears witness; its texts, almost throughout, are taken from the romantic poet Platen. They include at least three typical examples of what we may call Brahms's massive architecture: 'Wie rafft' ich mich auf in der Nacht', 'Wehe, so willst du mich wieder', and 'Nicht mehr zu dir zu gehn'. They suggest a renaissance of the antique, and recall the style of a Handel oratorio. The splendid 'Von ewiger Liebe', 'Ach, wende diesen Blick', and 'Willst du, dass ich geh' are others which belong to that category.

It is astonishing how, in all these songs, a firm grasp of classical style goes hand in hand with the most finely drawn characterisation and psychological insight; even more than in the others is it strikingly evident in 'Nicht mehr zu dir zu gehn' with its almost neurasthenic suggestion, inherent as that is already in the words. 'Willst du, dass ich geh' is of a wholly similar quality, and 'Von ewiger Liebe' might well be described as a love song of monumental power.

In all these songs, however, Brahms remains true to his romantic self; texts which are too realistic or which, like ballads, recount actual happenings, did not appeal to him. Even among the lyric poems, he selected those in which the romantic mood does not unduly stress any expression of intimate feeling.

This concentration on the romantic explains why, unlike Schumann, he preferred those Heine poems whose context is purely lyrical, whatever of bitterness may be implicit in the words. Brahms's songs on Heine texts are: 'Es schauen die Blumen', 'Mondenschein', 'Sommerabend', 'Es liebt sich so lieblich im Lenze', and 'Der Tod, das ist die kühle Nacht'. Among these songs of wonderful beauty, the last is, by common consent, the most valuable. What an achievement it is to have built it up, as Brahms did, on a single motive throughout, consisting of only two tones. Goethe is represented in Brahms's songs only by three out-and-out romantic poems—'Trost

FRANZ SCHUBERT
A posthumous portrait by an artist who was a close friend of Schubert
Oil painting by Wilhelm August Rieder, 1875. Schubert Museum, Vienna

in Tränen', 'Die Liebende schreibt', and 'Serenade'—and by the merry 'Unüberwindlich'.

Brahms was no lover of what has come to be called "tone-painting", and in most of his songs, as in his other music, shunned the imitation of bird-song or other sounds of Nature. Only once or twice in the merry or humorous songs, which he regarded rather as jests, did he swerve from that principle. When he did, he could achieve telling effects. In the Goethe song 'Unüberwindlich' (Irresistible), the drawing of a cork from its bottle is so vividly imitated in the accompaniment as to be brought almost visually before us; so, too, in the charming song 'Therese' the humming of a shell held to the ear, and in 'Salamander' the creature's dashing to and fro, are convincingly presented. We may not be far wrong in ascribing these occasional excursions into merriment to his having gone, about his thirtieth year, first only as a visitor, but eventually to settle there for good, to Vienna, the city where the joy of life once prevailed.

The city itself, where the very air was music, beguiling its people to a lighthearted zest for living, with the charm of its surrounding hills and woods, an ideal setting for outdoor delights, made from the very first an irresistible appeal to Brahms; he must have found some inspiration, too, in the thought of the country as having given birth to Mozart and Schubert and having drawn Haydn and Beethoven to adopt it as home. The laughing Muse, besides, of the bewitching waltz measures of Joseph Lanner and the Strausses must have helped to banish from his spirit the cares and shadows of his youthful days. No wonder that he now and then felt himself caught in the toils of music's gayer moods, and wrote waltzes of his own for pianoforte and for vocal quartet with pianoforte accompaniment—the two cycles of *Liebeslieder-Walzer* (Love-Song Waltzes), opp. 52 and 65. They capture the spirit of the Viennese waltz measure with charming success, and each has more than one effective song for a single voice.

The nearness of Hungary, moreover, gave him opportunities for widening his knowledge of the temperamental Hungarian and Gipsy music for which, even in his younger days, he had discovered some affinity in himself; to its influence he owed the inspiration not only of his Hungarian Dances and Gipsy songs but of many another in which some echo of Hungarian music can be heard.

But above all it was the city of Vienna with its long tradition of culture and many-sided interest, its noble buildings and gardens, its surrounding fairyland of hill and lake, which roused his inspiration and his innate love of Nature to their loftiest height. Many of his most splendid songs bear

'SAPPHIC ODE'
Part of Brahms's original manuscript, c. 1883

witness to this. As one instance 'Feldeinsamkeit' is a magical evocation of idyllic peace and of a spirit merged in Nature's own. No one has expressed that in nobler music than Brahms.

So, too, in the introduction to the song 'Unbewegte laue Luft', the soundless quietude of Nature is vividly depicted. How many such masterly songs there are for which Nature was the inspiration: 'O kühler Wald', 'Die Mainacht', the noble 'Abenddämmerung', 'O komme, holde Sommernacht', 'Auf dem See'. Besides these are the many enchanting bird-songs, above all the witchery of 'Nachtigall' ("O Nachtigall, dein süsser Schall"), and 'Lerchengesang' with its ethereal tones falling on us seemingly from the skies. These are in truth heavenly songs; they have, besides, an interest of their own in being composed in part in recitative manner. There we have one piece of evidence of the importance he attached to declamation in music; only seldom did he allow his attachment to a musical line to stultify it.

In the songs we owe to his later years, there are many revelations of his skill in welding a musical phrase and perfect declamation into a melodious unity. Among other noble songs for which I cherish a profound love and admiration, though I have always felt that I may not sing them—composed as they are without exception for the deeper men's or women's voices— are some in which Brahms unquestionably reached the loftiest summit of his song creation. To name only a few of them, 'Todessehnen', 'Ein Wanderer', 'Steig auf, geliebter Schatten', 'Mein Herz ist schwer' and finally the *Vier ernste Gesänge*, must be counted as among the most precious and profoundly moving in the whole literature of song. The last-named are settings of texts from the Old and New Testaments; they may well stand as a summing-up of all that Brahms's heart and spirit bequeathed to us.

GESELLSCHAFT DER MUSIKFREUNDE, VIENNA
The Society's old building in the Tuchlauben. Engraving, 1837

V

THE WORDS COME FIRST

RAHMS had already composed a number of his most important B works, and was winning his world-wide recognition, when Hugo Wolf, his junior by twenty-seven years, was beginning to make a name for himself, first as music critic on one of the less important journals in Vienna, and a little later as a song composer.·

His whole musical career falls within the period when the world of music was holding its breath over the revolutionary works of Wagner's genius, when music's younger spirits, especially, were being carried away on a wave of frenzied enthusiasm. When Wagner came to Vienna in 1875 to rehearse and produce *Tannhäuser*, the fifteen-year-old Hugo Wolf fell straightway under the spell; as he wrote in a letter at the time, "I became an enraptured Wagnerite overnight."

Till then his essays in composition had been only pianoforte pieces, but before long he was beginning to compose songs; inevitably they betray some influence of Wagner. Though they undoubtedly show real musical gifts, they are, for the most part, obviously a beginner's efforts; not till thirty-three years after his death were they published, though that was known to be against his own wish. One or two of them, however, did appear in his life-time, and at once revealed unmistakable signs of genius. First place among them must be accorded to 'Mausfallensprüchlein'; like 'Zur Ruh, zur Ruh', it comprises within its brief compass almost all the distinguishing characteristics of Wolf's genius. Creative maturity is revealed in these two early songs, as unmistakably as in the very first songs of Schubert or Brahms.

The two cradle-songs belonging to the same period, as well as 'Morgentau', 'Die Spinnerin', 'Das Vöglein', 'Das Kind am Brunnen', and 'Über Nacht', all of them composed somewhat earlier, are beginnings of a rich promise. The 'Mousetrap' song, composed in Wolf's twenty-second year, is already an achievement of undoubted mastery. Exceptional gifts of melodic invention, flawless musical declamation, blended with a background of engaging charm in the pianoforte part, make up an incomparably deft characterisation of the child and the little mouse. The song—the first Mörike poem which Wolf set to music—is among the most widely loved in the whole literature.

In 'Zur Ruh, zur Ruh' (To Rest, to Rest), a contrasting note is sounded, lending a new and profound feeling to Kerner's noble poem. It may be

HUGO WOLF
Photograph, c. 1889

regarded as rounding off Wolf's youthful work; there was an interval of three years before the next songs appeared, and they have their rightful place among the creations of his maturity.

But before embarking on any discussion of them, it is essential, in order that Wolf's work may be seen in its true light, to dispose of the widely held but wholly false opinion that he was one of the musical progeny of Wagner—"the Wagner of song" as many a contemporary dubbed him.

On that theme many a heated discussion flared up, in speech and in print, in Wolf's lifetime. That a number of his songs do bear traces of Wagner's influence is no sound evidence for so wrong a verdict; among the hundreds of them there are no more than a dozen or so of which that can fairly be said, enough of itself, one might think, to demolish any support for the "Wagner-descendant" legend. Quite apart from the fact that the true Wagner disciples hardly ever turned aside, even in a single bar, from the model they were copying (it may be that they did not wish to), it is my firm conviction that a song composer simply cannot be a follower of an operatic dramatist. Had it been true of Wolf, his one work for the stage, *Der Corregidor*, must have turned out in the style of Humperdinck or Siegfried Wagner.

There must be some other reason for such a belittling of Wolf's renown, and it is easily discovered in the fierce controversies about his songs which made their way into print during his own lifetime. For years on end musicians, critics, and all the ardent devotees of music failed completely to discern wherein lay what was new in the idiom of Wolf's songs. He was known to be a fervid adherent of Wagner's principles, and as several of his songs did show traces of Wagner's manner, it was easy to jump to the conclusion that everything that seemed like an innovation in his art had been learned from Wagner. The flawless musical declamation, the deep meaning imparted to the words, the orchestral style of many of the accompaniments, these features he was accused of inheriting from Wagner; the music-drama elements of Wagner, so it was said, had been transplanted into song by Wolf. Only after his death did the more enlightened music critics point out, and stress the fact, that all those features of Wolf's songs were to be found in greater or less degree in many of the songs of other composers, and that he was accordingly no revolutionary innovator, but rather the master who had, more than any other, carried every factor in the craftsmanship of song-writing to its ultimate perfection. More than any of his predecessors, he had imparted a full significance to the poetic element, that is the words, and was thus the true creator of the so-called "Word-Tone-Song".

That is borne out by a letter of Wolf's to Humperdinck as the latter was on the point of bringing out an essay on the Wolf songs: "I beg of you, cast your net wide; give an historical abstract of the growth of song, and demonstrate the need for creative work like mine. Above all, let poetry appear as the mainspring of my musical idiom, for that is the root of the matter." And as the first editions of his Mörike songs were in the publisher's hands, he insisted that the title-page should read, "Poems by Eduard Mörike, for a single voice and pianoforte by Hugo Wolf". This indeed expressed his creed as a creative artist, and no mere wish to be hidebound by any convention.

Let me return now to the stage in his song-composing when a blank interval of three years followed 'Zur Ruh, zur Ruh'. In the next two years only ten songs appeared. The first few—'Der König bei der Krönung',

EDUARD MÖRIKE
Lithograph after Bonaventura Weiss, 1888

'Biterolf', 'Wächterlied auf der Wartburg', 'Wand'rers Nachtlied', and 'Beherzigung'—are remarkable works, though obviously influenced by Wagner, and no true instances of creative self-assurance. In the following songs, 'Der Soldat' I and II, 'Waldmädchen', 'Die Zigeunerin', and 'Nacht-zauber', on texts by Eichendorff, a sudden change of direction is evident, and Wolf's creative individuality, revealed already years before, in the 'Mousetrap' and 'Zur Ruh', comes to light once more. Especially is that true of 'Nachtzauber' (Night's Glory), which must be counted as among his most masterly and lovely songs. It appeared as the "up-beat", as we may call it, of the period of unexampled fertility on which he entered a few months later with the beginning of the Mörike series.

No fewer than forty-four of these songs were written in some three months. They are unquestionably the best he has given us; almost invariably several of them form part of song-recital programmes in any part of the world. Nowhere in them is there a sign of hesitancy, of inspiration having faltered; so great a volume produced at such speed is of itself a giant's achievement, and the songs display a versatility which surpasses even Schubert's. A few months later nine further Mörike songs were added to the series.

Their poems cover well-nigh the whole range of mankind's experience, amid his homely joys and sorrows, or face to face with Nature's self, love's emotions and love scenes, tragedy and comedy, portraits, landscapes, caricatures, worship and prayers, in a word the whole realm of actuality and fantasy. Oddly enough there is only one song of tragic import—'Ein Stündlein wohl vor Tag'—among the first fifteen Mörike songs; it looks as though Wolf had deliberately turned first to the more lighthearted poems as a balm for his own spirit, darkly clouded as it had been by more than one experience, above all by the loss of his father.

The very first song, 'Der Tambour' (The Drummer), is one of infectious humour and deft miniature-painting. So, too, is the charming 'Jägerlied' (Huntsman's Song) with its graceful 5/4 measure suggesting the hopping bird. Then there is the brilliantly effective 'Nimmersatte Liebe' (Insatiable Love) with its perfect stressing of every word and tone, and the middle section's soaring emotion. How impressive is the way in which the opening words "So ist die Lieb'" are presented differently in their repetition, with the note on the word "die" lengthened. The deliberate banality of the melody to the last words, "Und anders war Herr Salomo, der Weise, nicht verliebt", and the noble closing bars form a contrast of great charm, emphasising the guileless hint of indelicacy in the text.

Other songs of incomparable mastery are 'Zitronenfalter im April', where the fluttering of wings is almost visually set before us, 'Elfenlied', and 'Waldmädchen' with its touch of genius in the depiction of the almost noiseless tripping to and fro of elves. In 'Der Gärtner' (The Gardener) it is above all the grace of rhythm which is captivating, with the Princess's stately mien and the little horse vividly presented. No less successful in their characterisation of the words are the delicate chromatic passages of the pianoforte in 'Nixe Binsefuss', tender as a caressing breath of wind, and in the charming 'Begegnung'. Similarly in that incomparable stroke of genius, the 'Lied vom Winde', it is the chromatic runs in the accompaniment which depict the tender sighing of the wind with convincing illusion.

One of the most poetic among the Mörike songs is 'Das verlassene Mägdlein' (The Forsaken Maiden), a poem of which we have also a setting

'AN EINE ÄOLSHARFE'
Autograph album leaf, 1888

by Schumann. The two are remarkably alike, a fact which suggests that Wolf had been unable to forget the impression Schumann's song had made on him. A letter to a friend shows with what a modest reverence he compared his with Schumann's. He wrote: "I have just composed, without actually having intended to, 'Das verlassene Mägdlein', of which Schumann had already written a heavenly setting. I composed it almost against my will, but perhaps just because I let myself be carried away by the magic of the poem, something outstanding has emerged, and I think my song is fit to take its place beside Schumann's." The beautiful Mörike poem 'Er ist's' has also been composed by both masters with a like perfection.

The wholehearted love of Nature's moods which fills many of the Mörike lyrics was clearly the inspiration of songs like 'Fussreise' with its irresistibly sunny spirit, and the splendid 'Auf einer Wanderung', in which a sense of glorious colour is developed. In the middle section Wolf sets

◆ 47 ◆

before us the purple of the skies, the rippling stream, the mill, and the city as we turn to look back on it, as only genius can.

In all these songs Wolf's romantic leanings are easily discerned; they were obvious already in 'Nachtzauber'. The Mörike 'Heimweh' ("Anders wird die Welt") is another of such deeply felt songs, full of the true romantic spirit. With what simplicity has Wolf set the words "Fort, nur fort, die Augen geh'n mir über"; it is a passage which can indeed bring tears to the eyes. And what an amazing wealth of tone-painting there is in the song 'In der Frühe'; we seem actually to hear the church bells chiming as we merge our spirits in the solemnity of morning's mood.

The elegiac feeling of that song is almost surpassed by the more than earthly beauty of 'Im Frühling' and 'An eine Aolsharfe' with tones of enchantment in its accompaniment. Brahms's song of the same title, despite its undeniable beauty, is left somewhat in the shade beside it. Among such elegiac songs are the two popular settings, 'Verborgenheit' and 'Weylas Gesang', as well as 'An die Geliebte' which is only seldom heard though it has such spirituality and depth of emotion as might set it apart in a place all its own.

The tragic Mörike songs, too, are in truly elegiac mood, forming a striking contrast in that way with the more realistic Heine texts, where, for the most part, actual events or mood pictures are presented. Such an elegiac song is 'Denk' es, O Seele' (O Soul, Consider). How masterly is Wolf's grasp of the foreboding of death's approach, and the sudden outbreak of despair, and how overpowering at the close is the gentle thought of the nearness of death, in its funeral-march measure. We are reminded of the end of the third song in Schumann's 'Der arme Peter', where a like rhythm is sounded. 'Lebe wohl', too, and 'Seufzer' are songs of deep grieving; their tragedy moves us in the same way as do the devout 'Wo find ich Trost', and 'Auf ein altes Bild'.

But the humorous and grotesquely comic are also represented in the Mörike songs, notably in 'Storchenbotschaft', 'Bei einer Trauung', 'Abschied', and several others. And before taking leave of the Mörike songs, I must mention that important work, the ballad 'Der Feuerreiter'. It is best summed up in Wolf's own words: "Beside this song all my previous work is mere child's play. The music is so aptly characteristic and withal of such intensity as might shatter the nervous system of a block of marble."

When we compare Wolf's settings of Mörike with his other songs, we realise that no other poet was so wholly akin to his own spirit. Among his Mörike songs there is hardly one that can be called less than wholly con-

JOHANN WOLFGANG GOETHE
Drawing by C. A. Schwerdgeburth, 1832

vincing, while in other series an occasional weakness does now and then obtrude itself. How highly he cherished Mörike, besides, is clear from his having turned to him for his first songs, and setting an unbroken series of them. True, he kept to that principle later also, in his settings of other poets; it is that, no doubt, which we have to thank for the faithful way in which each song series reflects the individuality of its poet.

While he was still busied with the last of the Mörike songs, he began several by Eichendorff, but only a few of them were completed then. Not, it may be, on the same high plane as the Mörike songs, they do include a number of virile and characteristic pieces which have a real worth of their own. Among them may be singled out for special mention 'Verschwiegene Liebe', and the appealing 'Ständchen', in which Wolf has achieved an unquestionable masterpiece of self-contained song. One month after this he began the composition of the Goethe songs; in the course of little more than three months fifty-two of them were written in an unbroken series.

In the very first of his Goethe songs Wolf created a mood-picture of noble simplicity and beauty—'Anakreons Grab'. Goethe wrote his splendid poem after a visit to the Greek poet's grave, and its wonderful elegiac mood is enhanced in Wolf's setting. A no less effective mood picture is 'St. Nepomuks Vorabend' (St. Nepomuk's Eve). It may help its hearers if I give a brief explanation of its text. According to legend, the priest Nepomuk was thrown into the Vltava by command of King Wenceslaus IV of Bohemia, for refusing to betray a secret imparted to him in confessional by the Queen. As his body floated down the river, five stars were seen to shine about it. Nepomuk was canonised, and every year, on the eve of the anniversary of his death, lights are seen floating in the river, and the pealing of bells and the voices of children in chorus are heard. Goethe took part once in the annual festival which is observed on that evening, and it was that experience which inspired his poem; Wolf's setting is at once charming and eloquent of reverence. Other freshly lyrical songs are 'Frühling über's Jahr', 'Blumengruss', and 'Gleich und Gleich'.

All the songs from *Wilhelm Meister* are masterpieces of characterisation, and, for my part, I think the Mignon songs the most successful in that way, despite the hints they give of a conscious effort to mould them in true accord with Goethe's mind. The setting of Mignon's ballad 'Kennst du das Land', however, is masterly in every way.

Many things in the *Schenkenbuch* and the cycles of Hatem and Suleika songs reveal the gift Wolf had for opera composition; in my view he has let himself be lured in them from the ideals maintained so perfectly in his work as a whole. It would be idle to deny that in his Goethe settings Wolf somehow failed to give of his best—and that despite the way in which his genius could penetrate the spiritual atmosphere of the poems. It may be that the individualities of the two men were too strong to allow their art to run, as it were, in double harness. But besides the songs I have cited above there are other exceptions, notably the three sublime poems 'Grenzen der Menschheit', 'Prometheus', and 'Ganymed', in all of which Wolf achieved convincing musical renderings of their well-nigh transcendental quality. Lastly I must mention that work of genius 'Der Rattenfänger' (The Ratcatcher), demonic as well as theatrical in effect; one can imagine how tellingly it could be performed on the stage in the manner of a Mephisto aria.

In the *Spanisches Liederbuch* (Spanish Song Book) which Wolf began immediately after finishing the last Goethe song, he found less opportunity

'THE HARPER'
Woodcut after Ludwig Richter for Goethe's poem from 'Wilhelm Meister'

for the display of his versatility; contrasts in that cycle are not striking. Except for the sections made up wholly of religious songs, the texts are almost all of erotic tendency, varying a good deal, none the less, in their presentation; lyrical, dramatic, grave, and lighthearted moods are all to be found in them.

In only a few has Wolf made use of local colour; the rhythms, on the other hand, suggest that many of the lyrics had their origin in Spanish folk-song. (The translators, or, strictly speaking, the arrangers, were the German poets Heyse and Geibel.) In the roguish or teasing songs particularly Wolf has introduced the effect of plucked mandoline strings in the accompaniments. Most attractive among these are, 'Sagt, seid Ihr es, feiner Herr', 'Klinge, klinge, mein Pandero', 'Seltsam ist Juanas Weise', and 'Auf dem grünen Balkon', to name only a few. In one of the most popular of all his

FROM THE 'SPANISH SONG-BOOK' (SECULAR)
Silhouette by Rolf Winkler

songs, one which he incorporated in his opera *Der Corregidor*—'In dem Schatten meiner Locken' (In the Shadow of my Tresses)—the rhythm alone is adapted to the manner of Spanish folk-song; in other respects it maintains the character of German song, largely by its avoidance of triviality.

The most valuable of the secular Spanish songs are without doubt those of serious import, composed as they are throughout in true German spirit. Among them may be cited 'Wenn du zu den Blumen gehst', 'Wer sein holdes Lieb verloren', and the effective mood-picture 'Sie blasen zum Aufmarsch' with its operatically conceived middle section, as well as the two tragic songs, 'Tief im Herzen trag ich Pein', and 'Komm, o Tod'. Finally, let me select the two dramatic songs, 'Wehe der, die mir verstrickte meinen Geliebten', and 'Geh, Geliebter, geh jetzt', which may well be counted as the most important of this series. The last, in particular, is a love song, or rather a love scene, of enthralling effect. That some kinship with the love scene in *Tristan* can be traced in its middle section is in no way distracting; it serves rather to enhance its effect.

The sacred songs, which appeared as the first of the series, no doubt form the most valuable part of the *Spanish Song Book*. They are unique works of that kind, in no way comparable with religious songs of any other period or any other composer. Their texts, translations and arrangements of sixteenth- and seventeenth-century lyrics, reflect the Spanish Catholic outlook of the Middle Ages; Wolf has found music for them, and especially for those which are full of fervid ardour, that can profoundly touch the hearts and consciences of all who hear them.

Foremost among them are 'Mühvoll komm ich und beladen' with its thought of miraculous healing, and the two dialogues for the soul and the Saviour, 'Herr, was trägt der Boden hier?', and 'Wunden trägst du, mein Geliebter'. The daring chromatic and modulation effects in the last are among the most magical achieved in such a way since *Parsifal*. In both, though designed for only one singer, the two voices are so vividly suggested as to make a more telling effect than they could do if presented by two singers.

Among the tender and appealing songs in the series, I would give pride of place to 'Nun wandre, Maria', the words of the blessed Joseph to Mary on the way to Bethlehem. The upward and downward striding of the thirds in the accompaniment, with the bass marking the steps of the two as they go on their way, form an effective support to the song. There must be cited also the charming 'Ach, des Knaben Augen', and the cradle song of the Virgin Mary, 'Die ihr schwebet um diese Palmen', with its poetic illustration of rustling palms in the accompaniment, and its forcefully dramatic middle section.

The secular songs in the *Italienisches Liederbuch* (*Italian Song Book*), akin in more than one way to the Spanish, lay even less emphasis on local colour. Wolf was concerned mainly with giving musical expression to the many moods and characters of the poems, and he realised—it may have been purely instinctively—that a consistent use of local colour must impair the standard of the series; he composed most of them, accordingly, in what

FROM THE 'SPANISH SONG-BOOK' (SACRED)
Silhouette by Rolf Winkler

is best described as the German spirit. That he was right is evident from the neglect into which Jensen's settings of the *Spanish Song Book* have long ago fallen, along with those of Wolf himself in which he strove to underline the Italian character. They are without doubt the least successful songs in the series.

In many others, however, he has lent such warmth to the erotic side of the Southern temperament as almost to suggest that he had Latin blood in his own veins. Such are, for instance, 'Wenn du, mein Liebster, steigst zum Himmel auf', 'Dass doch gemalt all deine Reize wären', and 'Wenn du mich mit den Augen streifst'. The songs, too, in which lovers' tiffs and jealousy are the motives, belong to the same category, for example 'Wer rief dich denn?' Wolf composed it in recitative style, and several nuances of light and shade make it engagingly clear that he conceived the song as telling of only an innocent little thought of jealousy. What a charming contrast is offered by the tender and consoling 'Nun lass uns Frieden schliessen', well adapted as it is for singing immediately after the other. There are one or two in the style of 'Wer rief dich denn?'—for instance, 'Hoffärtig seid Ihr' and 'Nein, junger Herr'—which are not so successful; Wolf was now and then over-careful of his musical line at the expense of the declamation.

Not always, however, in these songs are innocent or harmless thoughts of jealousy the motive. It sometimes assumes a graver form, as in 'Lass sie nur gehn, die so die Stolze spielt' (Let her begone! she acts with such disdain), and rises even to a terrifying height in 'Verschling' der Abgrund meines Liebsten Hütte' (May chasms engulf the cottage of my love), which recalls Isolde's wrathful outburst in the first act of *Tristan*. But side by side with these there are several enchantingly tender love songs, among them 'Und willst du deinen Liebsten sterben sehen', 'O wär dein Haus durchsichtig wie ein Glas', or the peaceful 'Sterb ich, so hüllt in Blumen meine Glieder'. Particularly effective are the roguish songs, 'Du denkst mit einem Fädchen mich zu fangen', and 'Ich hab in Penna einen Liebsten wohnen', with its wild high spirits, as well as one or two of boisterous comedy, like 'Ihr jungen Leute' and the rather indelicate 'Geselle, wollen wir uns in Kutten hüllen'.

From the songs composed in the last years of his life, I am tempted to select only the mood-picture 'Wie glänzt der helle Mond', clearly stamped as it is by his genius, and the three Michelangelo songs; these reveal him at the height of his creative maturity, intellectual as well as musical.

I have called his work "immortal" and "gigantic"; no lesser words would suffice for the tribute I have sought to pay to his achievement.

SCHUBERT AND HIS FRIENDS ON AN EXCURSION NEAR VIENNA

Leopold Kupelwieser, the artist, appears with Schubert near the left edge

Water-colour, 1820. Schubert Museum, Vienna

VI

FREEDOM, MELODY AND FEELING

ICHARD STRAUSS's position is unique. No other great opera composer has won a foremost place in the realm of song. Wagner left only five songs, and they can quite fairly be regarded as mere echoes of his operas. Strauss is the first to show that a composer can earn distinction in two such opposite fields; his twofold achievement is amazing when we contrast *Salome*, *Elektra*, and many another gigantic work for stage or concert platform with his tender and lyrical songs, as perfect as any which we owe to the great masters in that domain. For many years past Strauss has had a place of his own in song-recital programmes, among those whose music is most often sung; many of his songs have won a world-wide popularity as great as Schubert's, Schumann's, Brahms's, and Hugo Wolf's.

Among those which a music-loving public regards as "typical" Strauss songs—contrasts as they are to some far finer and less often sung examples of his art—we have two of the first he wrote: 'Zueignung' and 'Allerseelen'. 'Zueignung' (Devotion) was the first to appear in print and, like 'Allerseelen' (All Souls' Day), it at once revealed its composer's creative individuality. Although both keep closely to the form of varied strophic song, they do more than merely hint at the expressive freedom, the buoyant melody and the depth of feeling (so clearly evident in the prelude and coda of 'Allerseelen') inherent in his genius. 'Georgine', too, designed on a similar plan, and the impassioned 'Geduld' in the same group, are astonishingly mature first essays. In 'Die Verschwiegene' and 'Die Zeitlose', which are likewise among his early songs, we find the first instances of a device of Strauss's own, of suddenly leaving the voice unaccompanied, or supported, as in recitative, by isolated chords, a device which greatly enhances the declamatory effect. It is turned to account again in the songs 'Nichts' and 'Heimliche Aufforderung' ("Verachte sie nicht zu sehr").

Two of his best-loved songs appeared in the next series: 'Heimkehr' (Homecoming) and 'Ständchen' (Serenade). In its simplicity and lyrical restraint the first almost reminds us of Brahms, but 'Ständchen', though a youthful work, has obviously studied effects and reveals its composer as in some ways an innovator. Strauss has not kept to the traditional style of older serenades with their accompaniments imitating plucked strings, but has written a pianoforte part of real charm to which the song owes much

RICHARD STRAUSS
Lithograph by Max Liebermann, 1919

of its popularity. Any youthful flaws in the declamation are too slight to be called lapses. So, too, in the no less popular 'Wiegenlied', many years later, and in the little-known but rhythmically interesting 'Wiegenliedchen', Strauss achieved novel effects, quite unlike other and more conventional cradle songs. The engaging 'Meinem Kinde' is essentially a cradle song, though it does not bear that title.

Among the songs of his early years must be cited 'Die Nacht', with its ethereal fragrance, 'All meine Gedanken', gliding past like a shadow, and 'Du meines Herzens Krönelein', like a folk-song in its make-up. The flower songs—'Kornblumen', 'Mohnblumen', 'Epheu', and 'Wasserrose'—have a magic all their own, like the 'Weisser Jasmin' (White Jasmin) of a later date, whose accompaniment seems actually to conjure up the enchanting fragrance of the flower. Again and again in the accompaniments Strauss wins unique effects; virtuosic as the pianoforte parts often are, they need never give the impression of overwhelming the voice, so long as they are sensitively played. One song which stands out above all others in that way is 'Einkehr'. With what poetic feeling and what witchery of pianoforte passages does it present the twittering birds at their banquet in the boughs above us!

In the same way the songs 'Cäcilie' and 'Heimliche Aufforderung' win our affection largely by their attractive accompaniments. In 'Cäcilie', whose melody pours out like a stream, a wholly original effect is attained by varying the musical phrase for the first words, "Wenn du es wüsstest", at each of its six repetitions; the shades of meaning in the words are thus made to speak for themselves. No less effective is the man's song 'Heimliche Aufforderung' in which the soaring voice part is borne on streams of pianoforte arpeggios. Also set for a deep voice, 'Ruhe, meine Seele' is among the most nobly conceived songs of the same group.

What a striking contrast is 'Morgen', also in the same group! It is unique in the whole range of song, with a mystical, indefinable beauty over-lying it. 'Traum durch die Dämmerung', belonging to the following group, and the similar song 'Freundliche Vision' of a later date, likewise among the most often heard of the Strauss songs, are no less finished masterworks of classic perfection. In the song 'Schlagende Herzen' Strauss has given us an unsurpassed model of the recitative style, which is the hall-mark, too, of many another like 'Herr Lenz', 'Muttertändelei', 'Hat gesagt, bleibt's nicht dabei', and a number of those for a man's voice, such as 'Für fünfzehn Pfennige', and 'Bruder Liederlich'.

In 'Hat gesagt' Strauss has given us a brilliant setting of the popular humour of *Des Knaben Wunderhorn*, the famous early-nineteenth-century collection of German folk-song texts, and in 'Muttertändelei' (Mother's Dandling) the lovely melodic line of the song accords perfectly throughout with the spoken accent of the words. It is an instance, like a good many other Strauss songs in lighthearted mood, of the adoption of a dance-like measure; this can be found, too, in a number of Schubert's and Hugo Wolf's songs. It may be that it betrays some kinship between the Bavarian Strauss and the two Austrians. It comes to light most clearly in the song 'Ich schwebe' (I hover), which one can well imagine being sung with a swaying dance movement. But even in Strauss's broadly conceived songs, something of the same manner can be discerned; 'Glückes genug', for instance, has the cradle-rocking rhythm of a Viennese melody. Schubert and Wolf, indeed, set many a sorrowing or wistful text to music of just such a rocking

'DES KNABEN WUNDERHORN'
Oil painting by Moritz von Schwind, c. 1860

measure. Schubert's 'Der Müller und der Bach' and Wolf's 'Zitronenfalter im April' come to mind at once as instances.

One striking feature of Strauss's songs is that they are practically all settings of poems which no other composer has chosen. It looks as though he had deliberately avoided any which had previously been adopted. Unless I am mistaken, there are only two exceptions, 'Das Rosenband' which Schubert composed, and 'Waldesfahrt', one of Schumann's songs; the poets are Klopstock and Heine. The only great German lyric poets represented in his songs are Lenau, Rückert, Uhland, Goethe and Heine, and none of them by any great number. From Goethe he took only the little song 'Gefunden', three from the *Westöstlicher Divan* and the orchestral song 'Pilgers Morgenlied'. Not one of Mörike's or Eichendorff's lyrics has been set by Strauss. He has obviously been more attracted by the modern poets

Dehmel, Schack, Henckell, Dahn, Liliencron, and others of the time, and it is with their poems that he has unquestionably given of his best.

One point of interest is that not until his op. 56 did he turn to Goethe's and Heine's poetry—Goethe's 'Gefunden', and three of Heine's lyrics, 'Mit deinen blauen Augen', 'Frühlingsfeier', and the Christmas idyll 'Die heiligen drei Könige'. There is a suggestion of artificiality in 'Gefunden', a clear hint that Goethe's poem was not one which lay very near to Strauss's heart. In contrast to it, the feeling which flows so naturally through the Heine song 'Mit deinen blauen Augen' stamps it as one of his best inspirations. 'Die heiligen drei Könige', too, is an outstanding achievement, though it is only in the orchestral version which he arranged later that it makes its full effect. There are two others in the same series: 'Blindenklage' on a poem by Karl Henckell, and 'Im Spätboot' with its text by C. F. Meyer, which must be ranked among his most profoundly moving songs.

Only after an interval of fourteen years, the period when he was fettered in the toils of the operas *Elektra*, *Ariadne auf Naxos* and *Der Rosenkavalier*, did he turn again to song composition. Among the songs he wrote then there are four, designed for a high *coloratura* soprano voice, which I think are of more interest and value than the rest: 'Säusle, liebe Myrte', 'Ich wollt' ein Sträusslein binden', 'Amor', and 'Schlechtes Wetter'. In 'Amor' Strauss has given us a song of an order of which till then we had had only one other example—the recitative or declamatory *coloratura* song. Its difficulty, like that of the Zerbinetta aria, consists in the rival claims of *coloratura* virtuosity and clear enunciation of the words.

'LENORE'
Woodcut by Hermann Plüdemann, 1852

VII

THE WEALTH OF THE HERITAGE

N O other composer has left us such a wealth of German Song as Schubert, Schumann, Brahms, Hugo Wolf, or Strauss. That, I am confident, would be the unanimous verdict of the whole world of music. But it would be ungracious to end even so slight a book as this without some tribute of thanks to their predecessors and followers; many of them contributed generously to our heritage of song.

Goethe's affection for the music of Reichardt and Zelter, recalled in an earlier chapter, was shared by many admirers. Reichardt was a man of many parts, composer, conductor, author, and traveller, court musician at one period of his career to Frederick the Great and afterwards to Jérôme Bonaparte. His operas, oratorios, cantatas, and other music in the larger forms were widely performed, often under his own direction, in Paris, Berlin,

Vienna, London, and other centres. There is an amazing volume of them, and among the songs which win him a place of at least historical interest are some sixty settings of Goethe's poems. His daughter Luise, too, was at one time looked up to as a composer of songs.

Zelter's fame rests largely on the belief, none too well founded, that he was the originator of the *Liedertafeln,* singing clubs for men, which flourished throughout Germany. For some years Director of the Berlin Singakademie, he founded also an Institute for the study of church music, and remained at the head of it till his death in 1832. Any interest his songs once had was long ago eclipsed by the publication, in six volumes, of the letters which Goethe and he exchanged, and his music is no longer heard.

Zumsteeg, like Reichardt, also had a daughter whose songs enjoyed a vogue of their own. His name is remembered chiefly because Schubert as a boy was a warm admirer of his songs; his ballads, too, like 'Lenore' and 'Knight Toggenburg' were well known to Schumann and Loewe, and may well have had some influence on their work. He left eight operas, and among his other music are choruses from Schiller's *Die Räuber.* Schiller and he had been schoolfellows.

Spohr, one of the greatest of violinists, left ten books of German songs amid so much other music that a catalogue of it forms a bulky book by itself. Concertos and other pieces for his instrument will no doubt be treasured as long as the violin is played, and a good deal of his chamber music is still popular with amateurs. His operas and oratorios are still heard; one at least, *The Last Judgment,* is better known in England than in his own country. But few of his songs won any lasting popularity; 'Rose softly blooming' and 'The Bird and the Maiden' are almost the only ones known to singers of to-day.

In speaking of Richard Strauss as the one great composer of opera and song, I had not forgotten Weber. The first of the "romantic" opera composers, he left a great deal of music in other forms, and it includes nearly a hundred songs for one or more voices with accompaniments for pianoforte or guitar, and some with choruses; but no one sings them now. Born two years later than Weber, in 1796, Loewe too was a composer of operas and oratorios, in several of which both he and his wife took part as singers. But it is his ballads which won him his high rank, and many of them are destined to have an enduring place in the affections of singers. A complete edition of them fills eight volumes.

Mendelssohn's best music for voices went into his oratorios, *Elijah* and *St. Paul,* and many another work where solo and concerted numbers show

'SWEET ROSE THAT GROW'ST O'ER HER TOMB'
English edition (1848) of Loewe's 'Die Grabrose'

how wholly he was master of the effects that voices can produce. He left some seventy songs, a few of which are still quite often heard, though it is no disparagement of them to say that they have been elbowed into the background by the popularity of his *Songs without Words* for pianoforte. The hymn 'Hear my Prayer' for soprano, choir, and organ or orchestra (the orchestral version was an afterthought) is no doubt the piece which the world at large associates with the name of Mendelssohn; as a gramophone record with a boy's treble taking the soprano part it has been a best-seller.

His friend Hiller, like him a son of Jewish parents, was also more interested in the larger forms of music, though he did write a number of songs. His contributions to the literature of music are valuable, and he was on the best of terms with all the great people in the music of his day. The outstanding composer of songs among them was Robert Franz; some critics accord him a place beside the great masters. Schumann and Liszt were among his admirers from the first, and it is a testimony to the regard in which he was held, that Liszt, Joachim, and others raised funds to help him in his latter days when deafness and ill-health overtook him. His songs, simple and unaffected, often reminding us of folk-song, have won him a secure place in German hearts for all time. There are more than two hundred and fifty of them.

His contemporary Franz Abt enjoyed as great a popularity in our grand-fathers' days, and one or two of his songs have an abiding place of their own along with the traditional folk-songs. Founder and conductor of more than one choral society, in Switzerland and in his own country, he endowed them with a rich store of part-songs, numbering some hundreds, mainly for men's voices; without pretending to any depth of feeling or much originality, they are well adapted for singing as an outlet for good spirits, for making a joyful noise. He was one of the early German invaders of American concert platforms; accepting an invitation from several United States choral societies in 1872, he was there given the warmest of welcomes.

Cornelius and Humperdinck may be named together though thirty years separate their birthdays in 1824 and 1854. Each is best remembered by one opera (though in neither case an only opera), *The Barber of Bagdad* and *Hänsel and Gretel*; both contributed to the literature of music, and each, in his own day, was a sturdy supporter of Wagner. Cornelius was one of the "New German School", as it was called, which rallied round Liszt at Weimar, and he remained a lifelong friend of his master. Many of his songs are settings of his own poems; the best-known are the *Brautlieder* (Bridal Songs), a set of six, published after his death. Most of Humperdinck's purely vocal music

THE HUNTSMEN'S FAREWELL
Headpiece to Mendelssohn's 'Der Jäger Abschied'
Woodcut by Franz Pocci, 1843

is for men's or mixed voices, composed before *Hänsel and Gretel* won him his fame, and it never had the vogue achieved by that of Cornelius.

Half-way between these two in date of birth is Jensen, and he, too, composed an opera, though nothing was known of it till after his death. It is as a composer of songs that he will be remembered, tender songs of simple feeling, many of them to texts by Burns, Moore, Cunningham, Tennyson, Mrs. Hemans and Sir Walter Scott; like Hugo Wolf, he was attracted by the Heyse and Geibel translations in the *Spanisches Liederbuch*, and composed two sets of them.

Of a very different order are the forty-two songs by Mahler, the orchestral despot who was one of the outstanding conductors of his day, notably of the Wagner operas, in Vienna, New York, and other centres of music. Best known for his nine symphonies and his *Das Lied von der Erde*, he is looked upon in Germany as one of the last of the classical-romantic composers, carrying on the tradition of Brahms with something of Wagner's influence.

The tradition bids fair to defy the assaults of new tone systems, whole-tone, twelve-tone scales and other revolutions, and is worthily upheld in our own day by Hans Pfitzner, Max Reger, and Josef Marx; all of them, in their songs at any rate, are romantics at heart, with whatever angularity or seeming pedantry they choose to express it. Erik Meyer-Helmund should be mentioned, too, not only for the grace and delicacy of his songs, but as a rare instance of the union of three forms of art: poet (many of his songs are on poems of his own), composer, and singer. He had a distinguished career on concert platforms. Two operas and a ballet composed by him have also won successes.

My list is by no means exhaustive; many composers have contributed to the wealth of German song—a heritage which the whole word treasures. Our thanks, our homage to them have been given eloquently, but never more sincerely nor with a more warmhearted gratitude than these pages have striven to express. All that I would say is fitly summed up by Hans Sachs, at the end of Wagner's *Meistersinger*, as he tells the people:

> *Verachtet mir die Meister nicht,*
> *Und ehrt mir ihre Kunst.*
> ("Do not despise the Masters' ways,
> But honour well their art.")

'SPRING'

Robert Reinick's illustration for one of his own songs, 1874

VIII

ON THE INTERPRETATION OF SONG

IN spoken word, and on the printed page, much thought has been devoted to the interpretation of song. But what seem to me the most important aspects of the subject, which on that account I propose to discuss in this postscript, are often forgotten.

The criteria of success in the presentation of an opera or oratorio role are the quality of voice and vocal technique, musicianship and sense of style on the singer's part. But, besides all these, the presentation of a song demands something more which can never be attained by study, however long and conscientious, unless a natural gift is there as well. It is the gift of delivery or exposition; the gift of creating anew, by its union with music, the vision inherent in the poetry of the words; to bring it, as nearly as that is possible, visually as well as audibly before the hearer's senses.

It would be idle to ask me for any code of rules to that end; I do not believe that any such rules exist. My view is rather that the masterworks of song embody within themselves some secret powers; it is to the heart of these that we must seek to penetrate if we are to grasp their full significance. I heard the great Lilli Lehmann in one of her concerts when she was already an old lady, and no longer in full possession of her singing voice. But I shall never forget the impression made on me by every one of her song renderings. They were distinguished by a well-nigh incredible freedom of delivery, though the composers' intentions were always faithfully observed. Never for a moment had one any impression of rigid adherence to a rule; we were brought completely under the spell of her personality without being able to tell how this or that effect was attained. The two distinguished Dutch singers, Julia Culp and Johannes Messchaert, were likewise unsurpassed in that very way though neither had a particularly strong voice. Wherein then lies the secret of the impression made on us by the singer of a song? Or, to put it better, what is the secret by which a song, no matter how slight or unassuming, can be presented with complete effectiveness?

Let us consider Schubert's song 'Die Forelle' (The Trout), which every lover of music knows. I choose it for a brief discussion because it can reveal, more than any other, the art of a singer of songs. The words, though they have a charm and a thoughtfulness of their own, can hardly be said to have any deep significance; their content is simple enough for a child to grasp. The music Schubert found for it, despite its masterly appropriateness to the text and its taking pianoforte accompaniment, is among the less profound of his conceptions.

When we remember how many such songs flowed in a constant stream from his inspiration, we cannot be astonished that he never took time to add full indications of how he meant them to be sung. In 'The Trout' we have no more by way of such instruction than the general tempo mark and an occasional *p* or *f*. We can be quite sure, none the less, that he thought many a slight change of speed, many a stress, many a *diminuendo* or *crescendo*, essential. The song is often sung too slow, often too fast; Schubert marked it merely "*etwas lebhaft*" (somewhat lively), an instruction which many a singer interprets with a good deal of elasticity. But when we imagine the swift movements of the trout in the water ("da schoss in froher Eil' die launische Forelle vorüber wie ein Pfeil"—"there dashed in merry haste the freakish little trout, and vanished like a dart"), there can be no doubt for a moment of the appropriate tempo. Schubert obviously meant his "*etwas lebhaft*" to ensure that no one would ever take the song (as I once actually heard a singer do) "*quasi presto*". It is no less obvious that there must be

'THE TROUT'

Autograph written for Joseph Hüttenbrenner. After writing it down at midnight on
February 21, 1818, Schubert inadvertently spilt ink over the page

a slight slackening of speed at the point where the fish hangs on the angler's
hook. When the trout motive, which began in so merry a spirit, sounds a
little more tenderly and wearily in the accompaniment, and the pianist
carries that on in the brief coda, then the hearer is given an impression of
its pathos, slight and unassuming though the song may be. On the other
hand, it loses its value, and misses its effect, if it is either sung in an unvarying
monotone, or emphasised with exaggerated light and shade, or if the end
is presented too dramatically.

A very similar instance is the Brahms song 'Vergebliches Ständchen'
(Serenade in vain). It has suffered from so many inartistic performances
that it has fallen into some disrepute as a song of no great worth, as a thing
of almost shallow vulgarity. It is one of those which Brahms set, in accord

with its words, in simple folk-song style. The rustic character of the melody misleads many a singer into some monotony of performance which no more contributes to its effectiveness than the exaggeratedly pointed interpretation given by others, as though the piquant suggestions in the text—and there are several—brought it down to cabaret level. How far removed from any such thought was Brahms's conception of the song, is clearly shown in the many dynamic shades of expression indicated for its performance. Many singers apparently ignore them.

The lad's first words, "Guten Abend, mein Schatz, guten Abend, mein Kind" (Good evening, my sweetheart, good evening, my dear), are marked "*forte*" by Brahms. But immediately after them, "*piano*" is indicated for the pianist, and for the repetition of the words "Guten Abend, mein Kind". Why? Obviously because the girl has given the lad a sign to speak softly; for his next words, that it is love which has led his footsteps to her, and that she is to open her door to him, Brahms actually set the mark "*pianissimo*". The composer's meaning becomes clearer still as we notice that the words of the maid's refusal remain *pianissimo* till the lad, forgetting himself again in his disappointment, cries in a loud voice, "so kalt ist die Nacht" (the night is so cold), hoping to awaken the girl's compassion. But in the next moment, as at the beginning, "*piano*" is marked, which means that she has once more, by a sign, bidden him speak softly. That "*piano*" remains to the point where "*lebhafter*" (more lively) is indicated, and from then onwards Brahms again wrote "*forte*", as the maid takes umbrage at the lad's hint that his love may grow cold, and bids him go, not caring whether others overhear her. But she does that in no tones of anger or harshness, rather teasingly instead, and so at the words "Löschet sie immerzu" (let it be quenched, for all I care), to the merry pianoforte epilogue, "*p*" is once more indicated.

From these two examples we can learn how important it is for a singer to penetrate to the heart, not only of the meaning of the words, but of the music as well, if the poet's and the composer's wishes are to be faithfully carried out, and the song given the full effect it is meant to have. As a first essential, the words must be enunciated as clearly as though they were declaimed in speech. To that end, the phrasing of words and music must go together hand in hand; breaks must be equally appropriate for both.

But a singer is often faced with a problem where the composer has devoted more loving care to his musical phrase than to the text, so that the punctuation demanded by the words will not do for the music. In such a case I think it best, whenever possible, to let the due declamation of the words take precedence; it was Hugo Wolf's principle that "the words come first, and music takes second place". A singer, accordingly, must breathe not when he is in danger of being out of breath, but where the words or the music call for a momentary pause. To sing very long phrases in one breath, merely to show off one's breathing technique, is an inartistic trick which singers must avoid. I once heard the whole of the third song of Schumann's *Dichterliebe* sung in one breath — acrobatics rather than art, to my mind. It is quite as bad a fault, of course, to breathe after every word of a phrase; not only does it betray a fundamental lack of breath control, but it obviously destroys the whole effect of the song.

These few remarks may perhaps give some idea of the subtle shades of meaning, and the infinite varieties of treatment, that have to be observed by any singer who would aspire to serve with sincerity and truth so noble a form of art.

INDEX

(The figures in italics refer to the pages on which the illustrations appear)